YOUR PET
IGUANA

A TRUE BOOK

by
Elaine Landau

Children's Press®
A Division of Grolier Publishing

New York London Hong Kong Sydney
Danbury, Connecticut

A green iguana

Reading Consultant
Linda Cornwell
Learning Resource Consultant
Indiana Department
of Education

Author's Dedication:
For Jerry, Bianca,
and Abraham

Visit Children's Press on the Internet at:
http://publishing.grolier.com

Library of Congress Cataloging-in-Publication Data

Landau, Elaine.
   Your pet iguana / by Elaine Landau.
      p.   cm. — (A True book)
   Includes bibliographical references (p.) and index.
   Contents: The green iguana — Picking out an iguana — Your iguana's
home — Feeding — A healthy iguana — You and your iguana.
   ISBN 0–516–20387–8 (lib. bdg.)   0-516-26267-X (pbk.)
   1. Green iguanas as pets—Juvenile literature. [1. Iguanas. 2. Pets]
I. Title. II. Series.
SF459.I38L35 1997
597.95—dc21
                                                         97–17311
                                                             CIP
                                                             AC

Contents

A green iguana
in the wild

The Green Iguana

Do you like big lizards? Would you like to have a green iguana as a pet? These animals live in the wild from Mexico to South America. They are also found on some Caribbean islands. And in recent times, wild iguanas have been introduced into warmer regions of the United States.

A green iguana is not your average pet. These excellent swimmers and climbers are completely covered with scales. A row of spines called a crest runs along their back from head to tail. Adult iguanas may be up to 6 feet (1.8 meters) long!

In some places, people eat green iguanas. But most people look at these animals

An iguana out for a walk

Iguanas are excellent climbers.

as pets, rather than as dinner. Today, green iguanas are the most sought-after reptile pets in the world.

But pet iguanas are not for everyone. These tropical animals need special care. In the past, many pet iguanas died because their owners did not know how to care for them properly. So before you say, "I wanna iguana," read this book.

Only green iguanas should be kept as pets, but several other kinds of iguanas live in the wild. Two of the most interesting iguanas live on the Galapagos Islands off the coast of South America. The marine iguana lives on the coast of the islands. It dives underwater to find seaweed to eat.

A marine iguana shares a rock with some crabs.

The marine iguana below eats seaweed on a rock.

Iguanas

The land iguana lives in the dry interior of the islands. It never goes near water. Even though marine and land iguanas live on the same island, they look very different. Each has adapted to its environment.

Land iguanas live in the dry interior.

A land iguana eats a cactus.

Picking Out an Iguana

Green iguanas are not common household pets, so buying one may not be as easy as getting a dog or a cat. You may have to call several pet stores before you find one that sells unusual pets.

You should never rush into buying a pet, and this is

Think carefully before choosing an iguana for a pet.

especially true with iguanas. Plan on spending some time at the pet store. You may want to visit several times.

Take a close and careful look at the animal you hope to bring home. Make sure it is healthy. Don't choose an iguana who lies still in its cage all the time. It is probably sick. Healthy iguanas are active.

Look for an active and alert iguana.

Color is another sign of the animal's health. Very young, healthy iguanas are bright green. Older iguanas are gray-ish-green. Pass up an iguana with dull, yellowish skin.

Check an iguana's claws for injuries.

The inside of a green iguana's mouth should be pink. Mucus or other fluids coming from its mouth could be a sign of illness. And be sure to check the iguana's toes, claws, and tail for breaks or other signs of injury.

Your Iguana's Home

You can keep a small, young iguana in a large glass tank. But your pet will need a larger living area as it grows. Green iguanas are active lizards. They do not thrive in cramped spaces.

Since iguanas are tropical animals, they need a warm

Adult iguanas need large cages.

environment. Some iguana owners fasten a heat-producing lamp to the top or side of the cage, but there are other ways to keep your pet's home warm. Ask the staff at your pet store about the best way to keep your iguana's cage at the right temperature.

An iguana basks under a heat lamp.

Iguanas need time outside their cages.

Iguana owners should allow their pets to roam outside their cages for a little while each day. Some owners have set aside an entire room for a full-grown iguana. And these iguana rooms may even have small, built-in pools!

In tropical climates, people often build outdoor housing for these pets. Of course, it is possible to keep an iguana without providing a fancy home. Just be sure your iguana gets the exercise it needs.

Iguana

Make your iguana's cage look like the animal's natural surroundings.

Iguanas spend much of their time in trees, so include a few sturdy branches. In the wild, iguanas like to rest on branches while basking in the sun.

Your iguana's home should also contain several plants and clean rocks. Do not expect living plants to last very long though. Your iguana will either eat them or crush them. You'll save money by starting out with artificial plants.

Furniture

Make sure the rocks have no jagged edges, and place them so that they cannot fall on your pet. Your iguana will use these rocks for climbing and relaxing—or even to hide behind.

Your iguana will like a few sturdy branches to perch on.

Rocks, branches, and artificial plants will make your iguana feel more at home.

Feeding

Adult iguanas eat mostly plants. They enjoy the leaves and flowers of the dandelion and sow thistle, as well as clover, alfalfa, bean sprouts, and hibiscus flowers. You may also feed your iguana grated carrots, sweet potatoes, cab-bage, pumpkins, cucumbers,

Adult iguanas eat mostly plants.

okra, boiled potatoes, and peas. Many iguanas love lettuce, but they should only be given small amounts. Lettuce is not an ideal iguana food.

In addition to vegetables, iguanas should be fed small

amounts of fruit. Apples, pears, mangoes, bananas, peaches, plums, cherries, and blackberries are good. Use canned fruit when fresh fruit is unavailable. Many iguanas are especially fond of fruit cocktail. Twice a week, sprinkle a multi-vitamin and mineral supplement over your iguana's food.

During their early growth period, young iguanas eat mostly insects. Although adult iguanas eat mostly vegetables,

Iguanas enjoy fruits such as bananas (left). A few insects, such as this cricket (above), will add variety to your iguana's diet.

they should also be fed a few insects. Iguanas eat mealworms, crickets, locusts, and beetles. You may be able to find some of the insects iguanas eat around your home. Many of them are also sold in pet stores.

An iguana's food and water bowls should be large enough for the animal to step into.

You will need two large bowls for your iguana's food and water. An iguana's eating and drinking dishes should be about as large as the animal itself. This is because iguanas like to step in their food and water before eating or drinking. Iguanas also bathe in their water bowls, so their water should be changed daily.

A Healthy Iguana

Iguanas usually stay healthy if they are properly cared for. But just in case, watch for changes in your pet's appearance and behavior. These are some of the more common problems iguanas experience.

Some iguanas get ticks or mites. These tiny creatures live on your iguana and make

Iguanas usually stay healthy when properly cared for.

it sick. Ticks are small bugs with eight legs that attach themselves to the iguana's skin. Remove a tick by grasping it with tweezers and gently pulling it off the pet.

Afterward, dab the spot with alcohol to prevent infection.

Mites are much smaller than ticks, so they are harder to find on your pet. But if you see a white, powdery dust on

Check your iguana's skin for ticks and mites.

your iguana, it probably has mites. The dust is formed from the mites' droppings.

To remove mites, soak the iguana in warm water. Do not put your iguana back in its cage until the cage has been thoroughly scrubbed. Some iguana owners then hang a small piece of an insecticide strip in their pet's home for a few days. Check with your veterinarian before using other tick and mite remedies.

Perhaps the most common injury to an iguana is the loss of its tail. An iguana can actually lose its tail on purpose. In the wild, an iguana may do this to escape from an enemy that has grasped its tail.

An iguana's long tail can be injured if it is handled improperly.

The tail of a pet iguana sometimes breaks off due to rough or improper handling. When an iguana's tail breaks off, it leaves a bloody stump. The wound heals by itself in time, but you can apply anti-septic to the area to prevent

Learn how to hold your iguana without injuring its tail.

infection. Your pet's tail will start to grow back in a few months. However, the color of the new tail will not match the iguana's body as well as its first tail did.

Tropical animals such as the iguana can develop respiratory diseases in colder climates. If this occurs, your pet may have trouble breathing. Your iguana may also have a runny nose, lose its appetite, and change to a dull-gray or yellowish

Look for changes in your iguana's color. A dull-gray or yellowish color may mean it is sick.

color. An iguana with a respiratory disease must be seen by a veterinarian immediately.

Pet iguanas can have other health problems. The pet store where you bought your iguana will tell you how to

36

handle minor things. If you are not sure whether a problem is serious, call your veterinarian.

If you think your iguana may be sick, talk to a veterinarian.

You and Your Iguana

Have you ever seen an iguana resting on someone's shoulder? Perhaps you've spotted a pet iguana on someone's lap. These are tame iguanas. They have been handled by humans since they were young.

When you lift your iguana, make sure you support the

Tame iguanas like to be handled by people.

When lifting an iguana, support it beneath its abdomen and front legs.

animal beneath its abdomen and front legs. Never pick up or hold an iguana by the tail.

If you are looking for a sweet, affectionate pet, an iguana may not be your best choice. Iguanas are not loving. When they climb up on your lap or perch on your shoulder, it's only to keep warm. Iguanas are cold-blooded animals—they rely on their surroundings to control their body temperature. Your body

Your body heat will help your iguana keep warm.

is warm—to these lizards, you are more like a heating pad than a friend.

But there are other reasons to have a pet iguana. They are quiet animals. They are also unusual looking. These lizards remind us of prehistoric beasts or storybook dragons. If you want a pet that looks a bit like a miniature dinosaur—and if you are willing to care for a tropical lizard—an iguana is the perfect choice.

An iguana makes a very unusual-looking pet.

To Find Out More

Here are some additional resources to help you learn more about iguanas:

 **Books**

Barnet, Norman S. **Dragons and Lizards.** Franklin Watts, 1991.

Conant, Roger. **Peterson First Guide to Reptiles and Amphibians.** Houghton Mifflin, 1992.

George, Jean Craighead. **The Moon of the Alligators.** HarperCollins, 1991.

Gravelle, Karen. **Lizards.** Franklin Watts, 1991.

Ivy, Bill. **Lizards.** Grolier, 1990.

Martin, Louise. **Iguanas.** Rourke Enterprises, 1989.

McCarthy, Colin. **Reptile.** Knopf, 1991.

Smith, Trevor. **Amazing Lizards.** Knopf, 1990.

Souza, Dorothy M. **Catch Me If You Can.** Carolrhoda Books, 1992.

Organizations and Online Sites

Acme Pet
http://www.acmepet.com/ reptile/

Includes useful information on all kinds of reptiles. Check out the pet library for articles on iguana care.

American Society for the Prevention of Cruelty to Animals (ASPCA)
424 East 92nd Street
New York, NY 10128-6804
(212) 876-7700, ext. 4421
http://www.aspca.org/

This organization is dedicated to the prevention of cruelty to animals. They also provide advice and services for caring for all kinds of animals.

Lycos Mini-Guide to Pet Care
http://www.lycos.com/ lifestyle/miniguide/petcare. html

A list of online resources relating to pets and pet care.

Petstation
http://petstation.com/ herps.html

An online service for reptile owners and anyone interested in reptiles.

Pet Talk
http://www.zmall.com/pet/

An online resource of animal care information.

Important Words

antiseptic a substance used to destroy germs that cause infection

basking relaxing in the warmth of the sun or another source of heat and light

crest a ridge on an animal's body

environment surroundings

insecticide a chemical that kills bugs

lizard a four-legged reptile that has a long, scaly body and a long tail

mucus a slimy substance that coats and protects the mouth, nose, and throat

respiratory having to do with the act of breathing

roam to wander about

thrive to flourish or do well

veterinarian a doctor who treats animals

Index

Meet the Author

Elaine Landau worked as a newspaper reporter, children's book editor, and youth services librarian before becoming a full-time writer. She has written more than ninety books for young people.

Ms. Landau lives in Florida with her husband and son.